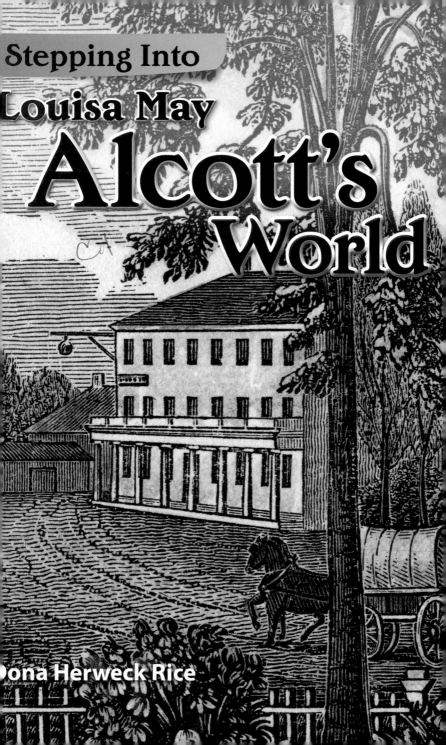

Stepping Into

Louisa May

Alcott's

World

Dona Herweck Rice

Consultants

Timothy Rasinski, Ph.D.
Kent State University

Lori Oczkus, M.A.
Literacy Consultant

Publishing Credits

Rachelle Cracchiolo, M.S.Ed., *Publisher*
Conni Medina, M.A.Ed., *Managing Editor*
Dona Herweck Rice, *Series Developer*
Emily R. Smith, M.A.Ed., *Content Director*
Stephanie Bernard/Susan Daddis, M.A.Ed., *Editors*
Robin Erickson, *Senior Graphic Designer*

The TIME logo is a registered trademark of TIME Inc. Used under license.

Image Credits: Cover and p.1 Old Paper Studios/Alamy Stock Photo; p.4 LOC [LC-DIG-pga-03789]; p.5 Project Gutenberg/Public Domain; p.8 Curt Teich Postcard Archives/Getty Images; p.9 (top) Stock Montage/Getty Images, (middle) Lebrecht Music and Arts Photo Library/Alamy Stock Photo; (bottom) Maryann Groves/North Wind Picture Archives; pp.11, 22 North Wind Picture Archives; pp.12–13 The Protected Art Archive/Alamy Stock Photo; p.12 Antiques & Collectables/Alamy Stock Photo; p.15 Mary Evans Picture Library/Alamy Stock Photo; p.17 Image used by permission of Louisa May Alcott's Orchard House; p.18 Niday Picture Library/Alamy Stock Photo; p.21 Internet Archive/Public Domain; pp.24–25 V&A Images/Alamy Stock Photo; p.25 Honolulu Art Museum; pp.26–27, 28–29 Bettman/Getty Images; p.30 Amoret Tanner/Alamy Stock Photo; pp.34–35 The Stapleton Collection/Bridgeman Images; p.35 Wikimedia Commons/Public Domain; p.36 Ed Isaacs/Dreamstime.com; p.41 LOC [ma0557]; p.42 Chronicle/Alamy Stock Photo; p.48 Houghton Library, Harvard University; all other images from iStock and/or Shutterstock.

We are grateful to Louisa May Alcott's Orchard House, the circa 1690 home where Little Women (1868) was written and set in historic Concord, Massachusetts, for reviewing the manuscript. For more information on the Alcott home, visit www.louisamayalcott.org.

Library of Congress Cataloging-in-Publication Data

Names: Rice, Dona, author.
Title: The world of Louisa May Alcott / Dona Herweck Rice.
Description: Huntington Beach, CA : Teacher Created Materials, 2017. | Includes index.
Identifiers: LCCN 2016026809 (print) | LCCN 2016044484 (ebook) | ISBN 9781493836192 (pbk.) | ISBN 9781480757233 (eBook)
Subjects: LCSH: Alcott, Louisa May, 1832-1888--Juvenile literature. | Women authors, American--19th century--Biography--Juvenile literature.
Classification: LCC PS1018 .R53 2017 (print) | LCC PS1018 (ebook) | DDC 813/.4 [B] --dc23
LC record available at https://lccn.loc.gov/2016026809

Teacher Created Materials

5301 Oceanus Drive
Huntington Beach, CA 92649-1030
http://www.tcmpub.com

ISBN 978-1-4938-3619-2

© 2017 Teacher Created Materials, Inc.

Table of Contents

"Too Fond of Books"...................4

Being an Alcott......................6

Civil War to Gilded Age..............10

Family Life..........................20

School Days..........................26

Clothing for Function and Fashion 30

Healthy Living.......................36

"Learning How to Sail My Ship" 42

Glossary............................44

Index...............................45

Check It Out!........................46

Try It!..............................47

About the Author....................48

"Too Fond of Books"

In the crisp days of autumn, a baby girl was born to Abigail (Abba) May and Amos Bronson Alcott, the second of their four daughters. The baby had dark hair, inquiring dark eyes, and an intense **kinship** with her father. She was born on his 33rd birthday, November 29, 1832. **Uncannily**, years later, they would die just two days apart.

Germantown Born

Alcott was born in Germantown, Pennsylvania, in an area that would later become part of Philadelphia. The family didn't live there long, though. In 1834, they moved to Boston, Massachusetts. Alcott would live in and around Boston for the rest of her life.

Boston Harbor, about 1841

4

Louisa May Alcott, as she was named, was the product of a world crafted by her brilliant and unusual father. She was in every way the child of her world, her time, and her place. And yet, in her own brilliance and determination, she too lived an extraordinary and unusual life. Some people said it was because she—like Jo, the heroine of Alcott's most famous book, *Little Women*—was "too fond of books, and it ha[s] turned her brain."

In the Alcott home, a fondness for books was not only a requirement but also something that one did unthinkingly, like breathing. A fondness for free thinking and questioning were also as natural as the blinking of an eye or the beating of a heart.

Could a person be too fond of breathing? Surely not. And in Alcott's world, books were the breath of life.

What's in a Name?

It was common in Alcott's time and place for children to be given not only their father's **surname** but also other family surnames as middle names. Alcott's sisters were named Anna Bronson Alcott, Elizabeth Sewall Alcott, and Abigail May Alcott. Bronson, Sewall, and May are all surnames on their family tree.

Being an Alcott

Bronson Alcott believed that people should live by their intellect. He was a noted Transcendentalist. Bronson and his wife, Abba, raised their daughters with these beliefs. They also surrounded themselves with other like-minded people, several of whom were quite famous and well respected. Many became Alcott's teachers.

The Alcott family was rich in friends and in the pursuits of new knowledge. But they were deeply poor financially. Bronson believed in living simply. He was a **vegan** before anyone used that word, and he thought a person should deny himself unneeded material goods. The family scraped by, often with the help of friends and benefactors. The three oldest girls worked to help support the family by cleaning, sewing, teaching, and taking care of other people's children.

Transcendent!

Transcendentalism was a popular spiritual and intellectual movement in the early 1800s. At its core, it suggests that all people and the natural world are good, and people create "evil" by corrupting nature and the natural state of things. Transcendentalists believe in:

- **self-reliance**
- goodness of humanity
- no religion and limited government
- equality and individual rights for all
- importance of the imagination and creativity

Despite continued poverty, Bronson believed in his ideals and methods for education. He started a school in which he talked with students and let them share their own ideas. This was shocking for the time! Students wrote and discussed their life experiences. They even spoke about their own interpretations of the Bible, an act that many found **blasphemous**.

Alcott and her sisters learned through these methods, but Alcott also had a mind of her own. She valued her own intellect—and she was fed up with being poor.

The Concord Circle

Alcott grew up among a group of intellectuals, philosophers, naturalists, and writers who shared Bronson Alcott's ideas. Some of them became Alcott's teachers, especially Henry David Thoreau. Ralph Waldo Emerson lived nearby and helped Bronson buy a house for his family. As Alcott grew and became a writer, she also became a welcome peer among this group of friends who lived in and around Concord, Massachusetts. Together, they became known as the Concord Circle.

Henry David Thoreau
author, naturalist, philosopher

"Go confidently in the direction of your dreams. Live the life you have imagined."

Ralph Waldo Emerson
author, poet, philosopher, leader of Transcendentalist movement

"What lies behind us and what lies before us are tiny matters compared to what lies within us."

Margaret Fuller
author, editor, women's rights leader

"If you have knowledge, let others light their candles in it."

Nathaniel Hawthorne
author, surveyor, diplomat

"Every individual has a place to fill in the world, and is important, in some respect, whether he chooses to be so or not."

Louisa May Alcott
author, **abolitionist**, **suffragette**

"We all have our own life to pursue, our own kind of dream to be weaving, and we all have the power to make wishes come true, as long as we keep believing."

Resting Place
Alcott is buried in a graveyard in Concord in an area called Author's Ridge. Thoreau, Emerson, and Hawthorne are buried there as well.

9

Civil War to Gilded Age

New England in the mid-nineteenth century was perhaps even more beautiful then than it is today. Bustling cities and slumbering towns were surrounded by deep forests and waterways. Alcott's life centered in Boston and Concord, Massachusetts. Because of this, her world and experiences were those of this **idyllic** place, despite her family's poverty.

A Time of War

The mid-1800s were also a time of great and growing tensions throughout the United States. In 1861, the tensions mounted to such a pitch that war between the Northern and Southern states broke out. At the root of the Civil War was the issue of slavery. Alcott and her family were abolitionists who believed firmly that no individual, regardless of race, should be enslaved. In fact, the Alcott home, Hillside, served as a station on the Underground Railroad. The Alcotts risked their lives and safety to bring enslaved people to freedom.

During the war, Alcott left home and went to Washington, D.C. There, she volunteered as a nurse, treating wounded soldiers. The heartbreak and horrors she saw became the topics of her book, *Hospital Sketches*. Civil War historians use her book as a reference for understanding the time and troubles of this bloody war.

Becoming Louisa

Throughout her twenties, Alcott used pen names instead of her own when she wrote purely for financial gain. At first, she was called Flora Fairfield and then A. M. Barnard. When *Hospital Sketches* was published in 1863, she began to use her real name.

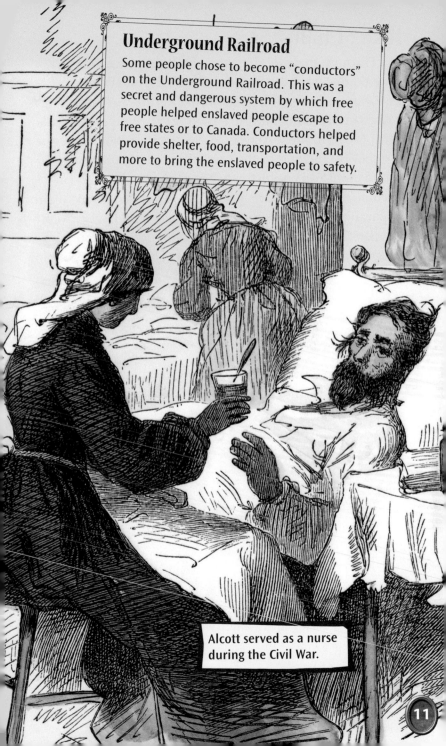

Underground Railroad

Some people chose to become "conductors" on the Underground Railroad. This was a secret and dangerous system by which free people helped enslaved people escape to free states or to Canada. Conductors helped provide shelter, food, transportation, and more to bring the enslaved people to safety.

Alcott served as a nurse during the Civil War.

Rise of Industry

Through the war, the North built many factories to provide materials for its war efforts. Several of those factories stayed in business even after the war ended. This helped create a big shift in American life and livelihoods. Prior to 1850, most Americans worked for themselves or farmed. By the end of the century, most people worked for an employer. In fact, a handful of businessmen became huge corporate leaders and **amassed** great wealth. Separation among financial classes grew and grew. Many families lived in terrible poverty, while a small group of people enjoyed lavish, golden lives. This time of economic and industrial change became known as the Gilded Age.

LITTLE WOMEN

Louisa M. Alcott

Two Volumes

Little Women is actually a novel in two volumes. The first, *Little Women*, was followed in 1869 by the second, *Good Wives*.

High Quality at Low Prices

The economic changes also saw enormous competition in business. The public demanded high-quality products at the lowest prices. Businesses scrambled to find ways to cut costs and drive competitors out of the market.

Big Boom

Despite the problems of Reconstruction and a huge **depression** in 1893, caused by overbuilding and bad financing, the U.S. economy nearly doubled after the Civil War.

The Alcotts firmly believed in self-reliance and fending for oneself. But the changing tides of industry were not in keeping with their beliefs. Bronson continued to struggle financially all his life. In 1868, Alcott published her most famous work. *Little Women* achieved great success and gave her financial independence. She found a way to use this to her advantage by becoming part of the ever-shrinking group of self-reliant people. For the rest of her life, she lived as a writer.

Little Women, Good Wives

Many girls today grow up knowing they have countless opportunities to do and become whatever they choose. Not so for Alcott and her sisters. Their poverty was their first restriction. They had to earn money simply to help keep the family alive, but the opportunities available to them were extremely limited. At that time, women could work as servants in wealthier houses. They could be seamstresses, sewing clothes for others, or they could be **governesses** or schoolteachers (usually, only if they were unmarried). Very few women worked in shops. Most women stayed in their homes to cook, clean, sew, raise the family, and care for the men.

Women were dependent on the men in their lives to provide for them. They had little or no opportunities to make money. Often, they were not allowed to own their own homes or land, especially if they were married (in which case, their property belonged to their husbands). If still unmarried past their early twenties, they were considered **spinsters**, or old maids, and it was assumed they would never marry. They'd be dependent on their fathers, brothers, and uncles throughout their lives. A spinster was a woman to be pitied.

Rights for Women

In Alcott's day, women could not vote or take part in government. That didn't change until 1920, when Amendment XIX to the Constitution was passed.

Beloved Classic

Little Women is the coming-of-age story of four sisters—Meg, Jo, Beth, and Amy—their mother Marmee, and their father, who is off at war. The family is modeled on Alcott's family. Jo, the character based on Louisa, is a strong, independent, hardworking writer who doesn't let society's beliefs get in her way.

Breaking the Mold

Alcott was fortunate. She was well educated, primarily by her father, and surrounded by an intellectual crowd of friends. Her brilliant and creative mind helped her carve out a career that very few women in the world could claim. She became a working, published, and successful author who was acclaimed and beloved for her skill.

Alcott never married, although she did receive one proposal of marriage, which she declined. She claimed she never loved a man, and her financial success meant that she could be independent. When Alcott's older sister, Anna, became engaged the same year that their younger sister, Elizabeth, died, Alcott considered both events tragedies and feared that the tribe of sisterhood would be abandoned forever.

Becoming a Writer

Alcott's first book was *Flower Fables*, published in 1854 under a pen name. She wrote it for Ralph Waldo Emerson's daughter. It and many other books and stories helped Alcott make a living until *Little Women* brought success and independence.

Motherhood

Alcott never had a child of her own, although at the time, becoming a mother was thought by many to be a woman's main role. Her sister Anna had two sons. After many years as a spinster, Alcott's youngest sister, Abigail (called May), married at age 37. Sadly, on December 29, 1879, May died six weeks after giving birth to her only child, Lulu. It was May's wish that Alcott raise Lulu. In this way, Alcott became a mother and aunt for the rest of her days.

Lulu's full name was Louisa May Nieriker.

THINK LINK

- How have women's roles and opportunities changed since Alcott's time?

- Are there any ways in which women's roles and opportunities are the same today as they were then?

- Do changing roles for women have any impact on men, and if so, how?

Declaration of Sentiments

In 1848, about 300 people attended the first women's rights convention in Seneca Falls, New York. Lucretia Mott and Elizabeth Cady Stanton organized the event where Stanton read a Declaration of Sentiments (modeled after the Declaration of Independence). Alcott read the declaration soon after and was inspired by its message.

A Vote for Women!

Beginning in 1879, Massachusetts allowed women to vote on town matters involving children and education. Alcott became the first woman to register to vote in Concord.

Fellowship

Abolition and women's rights often went hand in hand. Among the few men attending the convention in Seneca Falls was Frederick Douglass, a former slave and an acclaimed writer and speaker. He was an important voice in Alcott's time for an end to slavery and equal rights for all people.

Frederick Douglass

Here is part of the declaration read by Stanton. Following this section of the document was a list of grievances and 100 signatures.

We hold these truths to be self-evident: that all men and women are created equal; that they are endowed by their Creator with certain inalienable rights; that among these are life, liberty, and the pursuit of happiness; that to secure these rights governments are instituted, deriving their just powers from the consent of the governed. Whenever any form of Government becomes destructive of these ends, it is the right of those who suffer from it to refuse allegiance to it, and to insist upon the institution of a new government, laying its foundation on such principles, and organizing its powers in such form as to them shall seem most likely to effect their safety and happiness. Prudence, indeed, will dictate that governments long established should not be changed for light and transient causes; and accordingly, all experience hath shown that mankind are more disposed to suffer, while evils are sufferable, than to right themselves by abolishing the forms to which they are accustomed. But when a long train of abuses and usurpations, pursuing invariably the same object, evinces a design to reduce them under absolute despotism, it is their duty to throw off such government, and to provide new guards for their future security. Such has been the patient sufferance of the women under this government, and such is now the necessity which constrains them to demand the equal station to which they are entitled.

Family Life

Many New Englanders up to the mid-1800s had been tied to the demands of the farm and the season. There was little time for pleasure. New Englanders also mainly descended from **Puritans**, who did not value pursuits of pleasure. God, work, and taking care of responsibilities were their main values.

In Alcott's time, all this was still true. But as the farming society shifted to an industrial one, time demands changed for many people. Less farming often meant more free time to follow interests and enjoy family life. Greater industry also meant freedoms were added inside the home. For example, the invention of the sewing machine saved countless hours that would have been spent sewing by hand. Food and supplies made readily available in local stores saved people from growing and making their own.

In the past, families spent time together mainly during the cold winter months. In the evenings, they might have huddled around the fire, talking, reading, telling stories, playing music, or singing. Now, more and more families could enjoy these pursuits all year round. Many people learned to play instruments and shared music with families and friends. Telling stories and reading aloud well were treasured arts. And singing in harmony was a pleasure the whole family could enjoy.

A Woman's Magazine

Godey's Lady's Book was a monthly magazine with a huge **circulation** in the 1800s. It was filled with poetry, stories, articles, sheet music, and artwork. Each issue had one colored "fashion plate" of the latest fashion, often with a free sewing pattern!

GODEY'S
LADY'S
BOOK.

EDITED BY
MRS. SARAH J. HALE,
L. A. GODEY.
VOL. LXVI.
1863.

LOUIS A. GODEY
PHILADELPHIA

We can always supply back Numbers from January.

Hearty New Englanders

Even with changing times, most people in 1800s New England were able to make and do many things on their own. They sewed, knitted, baked, canned, wove cloth, raised livestock, mended fences, and even built their own houses.

Courting

When young men and women wanted to court, or date, there weren't many opportunities to get to know one another on their own. In fact, it really wasn't allowed. Relationships started under the watchful eyes of their families and often at church or church events. If a person showed romantic interest in another, he or she had better have serious intentions! Flirting without the intention of marrying wasn't allowed. Serious couples could court, but only when they were **chaperoned**.

Singing School

Singing schools became a popular trend in many areas. Local teachers or experienced singers would hold evening classes. Young men and women especially enjoyed them. The schools provided public places to see and get to know one another, enjoying a fun activity together.

At one time, marriages were arranged by a couple's families. By Alcott's day, people were marrying for love and through their own choices—but only with the family's blessing. When people decided to marry, they usually had long engagements. The man had to show he could provide for the woman and had to own a home. The woman had to build her trousseau. This was her supply of household items, including her clothes as well as sheets, tablecloths, aprons, decorative "fancy work," and more.

Wedding Bells

In the early 1800s, weddings were simple and took place at home. By midcentury, trends were changing. People sent **engraved** invitations to the events and were married in churches to make room for their many guests. Feasts sometimes followed the ceremonies.

Childhood

For much of history, there wasn't much "childhood" as we know it today. A child's responsibility was to help the family. Most homes didn't have playrooms, towns didn't have toy stores, and nobody had playdates.

Children were expected to spend their time learning everything they needed to know to become self-sufficient adults. Some children attended school but usually no further than the eighth grade. More boys than girls attended school. If children's support was needed at home, that took priority.

All children of Alcott's time dressed much like adults. Young children of both genders usually wore dresses. Boys' hair was styled similarly to their fathers' hair, while girls mainly wore their hair down, only pinning it up in their mid to late teens when they were considered to be women.

Let's Play Hoops

A popular toy of Alcott's time was a wooden hoop. Children could run alongside it, race it, roll it, twirl it, or rotate it around the waist just like children do today with plastic hoops.

Families spent much time together, often working side by side. Children saw friends at school or church, but their main playmates were their siblings. When they had free time, brothers and sisters used their imaginations to play games of all kinds. Typically, boys played more physical games, while girls played quieter, less active ones. Clear differences between boys and girls were strictly followed. Very few boys or girls—or men and women—dared to break from these **prescribed** roles.

Pink or Blue?

During Alcott's lifetime, people thought boys should wear pink because it was a bold and strong color, and blue was for girls because it was delicate. By the mid-1900s, these color ideas had switched. Today, all children may be seen as bold, strong, or delicate, and they can wear any color they like.

School Days

Massachusetts has been a leader in education since colonial days. All New England colonies required each town to maintain a school, mainly for boys. By Alcott's time, these were known as common schools. Children of all ages learned together in single-room schoolhouses. Older and more-experienced students assisted younger, less-experienced ones. Over time, more girls attended school.

Boston Latin School was the first public school in the United States. It was founded in 1635 as a grammar school (like a modern English high school), and it still exists!

Schoolbooks

The first schoolbooks in the United States had a strong basis in **morality**. By Alcott's day, *McGuffey Readers* had become the main textbooks. Each book in the series built on the skills from the previous ones, so students advanced through them at their own paces. These books were used widely far into the 1900s.

New England also set the trend for private high schools. These preparatory schools kept extremely high standards of education. Students were prepared specifically to enter college. Some of these **elite** "prep schools" still exist today.

Many schools required tuition or other fees. Such financial requirements created a clear distinction between rich and poor people, since many families could not afford the fees. It wasn't until 1870 that each state offered free schools, but these schools still were not available to all. Most schools were **segregated** and only allowed white children to attend.

College Bound

New England is known for its outstanding universities, many of which are the oldest in the United States. These include Harvard (founded 1636), Yale (1701), Brown (1764), and Dartmouth (1769).

Bronson Alcott speaks to a large group of students at the Concord Summer School of Philosophy.

A New Kind of School

Alcott's father often worked as a teacher, although he, like many other teachers of the time, had little formal education. Teachers were not trained with the same high standards used today, and many were self-taught.

In 1834, Bronson opened the Temple School. It differed from many schools of the day where students were taught to memorize and recite. Instead, Bronson taught them to analyze material and share and defend their thoughts. He also filled his classroom with items meant to inspire students, including books, artwork, and comfortable seating. People were both intrigued and puzzled. Bronson was forced to close the school when parents removed their children due to his unusual methods and beliefs.

Many other attempts to open schools through the years failed as well, often because of lack of funding. But years later, in 1879, Bronson opened a school for adults called the Concord Summer School of Philosophy. It was based on the teachings of the philosopher Plato. This school was a huge success. Adults (including women) from the United States and Europe came to study. Famous writers and thinkers were among its many speakers. Unfortunately, the school closed when Bronson died in 1888.

From Father, with Love

Alcott's father built the desk at which she studied and wrote. She wrote *Little Women* at this desk, which can still be seen at Orchard House (now a museum) in Concord, Massachusetts.

Clothing for Function and Fashion

Clothing of Alcott's era, called the Victorian era, was known for complicated layers and vast amounts of fabric—especially for women and those with money. The poorer classes and laborers wore layers but much more basic and inexpensive ones.

Short ankle boots were popular for men in Victorian times.

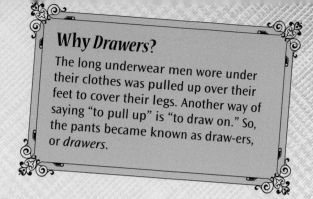

Why *Drawers?*

The long underwear men wore under their clothes was pulled up over their feet to cover their legs. Another way of saying "to pull up" is "to draw on." So, the pants became known as draw-ers, or *drawers*.

Men's Clothing

Men's clothing of the time consisted of undergarments, trousers, cotton or linen shirts, and cravats or neckties. A vest (or waistcoat) was worn over the shirt, and a coat finished the look. Earlier in the century, long frock coats were popular, followed by shorter sack coats, and finally, hip-length blazers. For formal occasions, men wore tuxedos. Men always wore hats outdoors, whether they were top hats, bowlers, or boaters.

What about pants? The word *pants* has an interesting history. A character named Pantalone is featured in an old Italian comedy. He was noted for the leggings he wore down to his ankles at a time when men wore leggings just to their knees. People called this style *pantaloons*, shortened to *pants*. But in the nineteenth century, *pants* did not mean what it does today. It was the word for men's underwear, also called *drawers*. The outer leggings men wore were called *trousers*.

Cravats

Men have worn neckties for centuries. Why? King Louis XIV of France admired the short red scarves worn by Croatian soldiers to tie the tops of their jackets. So, he made all men wear *cravats* (a French distortion of the word *Croate*) to royal events. The look stuck—even in today's fashions.

Women's Clothing

Victorian women wore layer upon layer of clothing. At the base was a cotton or linen **chemise** and stockings. Early in the century, some women wore pantalettes under the chemise, which were made of two pant legs attached at the waist (and why today's pants are called a pair); later in the century, women wore knickers. A corset was laced on top of the chemise to draw in the waist. Next, up to six petticoats, or one petticoat and a single hoop skirt, were added to give a dress fullness. On top of this was an overpetticoat with an embroidered hem. And all that was just underwear!

Over their undergarments, women wore long dresses with wide skirts, fitted **bodices**, long sleeves, and covered necks. Shawls could be worn over the shoulders. Outdoors, women wore bonnets or hats and gloves. For formal occasions, women sometimes wore open necklines, shorter sleeves, and more delicate fabrics. Gemstone earbobs and necklaces were common jewelry for those who could afford them.

The result? Victorian women could barely move, had trouble breathing, were easily overheated, and were exhausted from carrying about 20 pounds (9 kilograms) or more of clothing!

Don't Move!

The less a woman could maneuver, the greater the sign of her wealth. Moving in all those clothes wasn't easy, and such clothing took help to put on. Only the wealthy could afford to pay for this support, own so many layers of clothing, and spend days so inactively.

Hoop Skirts

To replace several petticoats and to keep a woman's legs free, hoop skirts came into **vogue**. Made of flattened steel wires that increased in circumference from waist to ankle, the hoops bounced back to shape after squeezing through a door or being sat on. At their peak, hoop skirts were about 6 feet (1.8 meters) wide!

Tight-Lacing

For centuries, many women wore corsets. In the 1820s, with the addition of metal eyelets through which strings could be threaded, the practice of tight-lacing began. A woman would have someone pull the corset strings as tightly as possible. The visual result was a curvy figure with a tiny waist. The physical result was great difficulty breathing. Women's back muscles became reliant on the corsets for posture. This caused back problems when the muscles relaxed. Some women even broke ribs when tight-lacing!

Bloomers

In the 1850s, the journalist and suffragist Amelia Bloomer made popular a new style of clothes for women. It was basically a full skirt divided in two and tied at the ankles. The balloon-like style was modeled after Turkish pants. Bloomer and others found them much easier to move in than the long skirts and petticoats women usually wore. But the public wasn't ready for such a change. Newspapers openly mocked and degraded Bloomer and the "bloomers" she wore.

The Queen's Knickers

Before the late 1700s, women usually didn't wear any type of underpants. In the 1800s, Queen Victoria became a fashion trendsetter. She was also highly reserved. To her, knickers (the underwear of the time) were essential. Soon, women everywhere wore knickers similar to the queen's.

STOP! THINK....

- Women often fainted when wearing corsets. Why?

- What might have been the appeal of wearing a corset?

- Why do you think women decided against wearing corsets in the early twentieth century as more of them began working outside the home?

women wearing bloomers

Healthy Living

During Alcott's lifetime, people became more aware of how **hygiene** relates to health. About 620,000 people died during the Civil War, but it is estimated that two out of three of them died of disease. What we know today of cleanliness and its relationship to germs was unknown in those days.

Historically, people did not bathe often. Water had to be carried into homes in large amounts, heated, and poured into tubs. That was a lot of work, and people didn't see the need for regular bathing. At most, they may have bathed once each week, often sharing the same bathwater used by other family members. During winter months, they'd bathe even less often.

Disease was rampant in the 1800s. Modern medicines hadn't been discovered yet and people practiced poor hygiene. People spread disease easily and unknowingly. Hospitals had no idea that cleanliness helped to keep away infection and the spread of disease. Patients and doctors did not regularly wash. Instruments and bandages were not **sterilized**. Germs and disease had ample opportunity to live, grow, and spread.

Death by Wallpaper

A common green dye in the 1800s included arsenic, a deadly poison. Everything from wallpaper to curtains to clothes may have contained the dye. No one knew that simply wearing a dress or sitting in a room could be fatal!

ARSENIC.
POISON

Short Lives

The average lifespan for men in Alcott's day was only about 45 years. Women's average lifespan was lower because of the risks of childbirth at the time. Many children died before age five. If they lived beyond five years, they had a good chance of reaching adulthood.

Terrible diseases such as tuberculosis, cholera, and smallpox often came in **epidemic** waves.

The Big Stink

Many people of the time, including medical experts such as Florence Nightingale, believed that bad smells caused disease. This had a lot to do with the fact that smelly, dirty cities (often filled with poor people) were fraught with disease, but sweet-smelling country towns (with few poor people) were disease-free by comparison. The upside of this belief is that experts urged cleaning to get rid of bad smells. The cleaning had the added unknown benefit of wiping out many germs.

Antiseptic

A doctor named Joseph Lister wondered why so many surgeries were followed by infections. He closely studied wounds through a microscope. He came to see that germs caused the infections. In 1865, he developed and used an **antiseptic** medicine. He also applied many layers of bandages to keep wounds clean. His treatment worked well. But doctors weren't quick to use his methods. It took many years for doctors to accept the germ theory of disease, even though it had been first proposed in 1546 and was later well defended by the scientist Louis Pasteur in the 1850s and 1860s. Most surgeons didn't widely accept Lister's treatment until late in the century.

Quacks

Poor people couldn't afford proper medical care. They relied on false medicines sold by street peddlers, called *quacks*, who were just looking to make money. The useless medicines promised miracle cures for everything from baldness to cholera.

Lady with the Lamp

Florence Nightingale is considered the founder of modern nursing. During Britain's Crimean War, she trained and organized nurses with great success. She became known as the "Lady with the Lamp," as she carefully checked on wounded soldiers at night, lamp in hand.

Louis Pasteur in his laboratory

The Fruitlands Experiment

Health was an important matter in the Alcott household. Bronson believed in pure food, water, exercise, and healthy, active minds. He saw to it that his children were raised with these principles as well.

Bronson didn't enjoy much success as a teacher until his final years, but he did have many followers. On June 1, 1843, Bronson and one of his admirers, Charles Lane of England, opened an experimental community. They called it Fruitlands, and they meant it as an "experiment in plain living and high thinking." The community was on a 90-acre farm in Harvard, Massachusetts. The plan was to have people live and work there, raising their own food and supporting themselves **communally**. Lane purchased the farm, and the Alcotts, Lanes, and a few other people moved there. Together, they planted eight acres of food and vegetation. They were practicing vegans who drank only water, used no artificial light, bathed in cold water, and used no animals for labor.

It was a big undertaking with good intentions for health and well-being. But it ultimately failed. The farming was too difficult and the winter too harsh, so Fruitlands closed after just seven months.

Redemption

The people of Fruitlands did not believe in owning land. How, then, did they justify the purchase of the farm? Lane said that he simply redeemed the land from its previous state of ownership.

"Transcendental Wild Oats"

In her later years, Alcott wrote of her time at Fruitlands in a short article called "Transcendental Wild Oats." The expression "to sow wild oats" means to do wild and even foolish things when young.

This image shows Fruitlands Museum, which is a cluster of buildings on the site of the original community.

"Learning How to Sail My Ship"

From birth, Alcott was challenged to be her best self. She accepted that challenge and carved a path of self-sufficiency, resilience, intellect, and work to create a better world. She was well respected and valued among her family, friends, and many readers. Writing was her outlet. It was also her road to financial independence and support for her family.

Despite healthy living, Alcott didn't live beyond middle age. For about 20 years, she suffered from a wide variety of symptoms, including fatigue and headaches. On March 4, 1888, she wrote to her sister that she wasn't feeling well. Shortly after, she became feverish and went into a coma. Alcott died on March 6, 1888. Experts today believe that during her service in the war, Alcott was exposed to mercury. For the rest of her life, she suffered the effects of mercury poisoning, and it caused her longtime ill health.

But in true Alcott fashion, Alcott's health challenges never stopped her. She was committed to a life of self-motivation and responsibility, and she lived it fully. As Alcott said, "I'm not afraid of storms, for I'm learning how to sail my ship."

Her many fans are so fortunate they can climb aboard that ship at any time and set sail!

THINK LINK

- In what ways was Alcott a product of her time?

- How was Alcott different from other women of her time?

- How would Alcott's life have been different if she had been a man?

Glossary

abolitionist—a person who wanted to stop slavery

amassed—grew or developed

antiseptic—a substance that prevents infection in a wound

blasphemous—showing disrespect to God

bodices—the top parts of dresses

chaperoned—being attended by another person in a social setting, especially during courtship

chemise—a woman's undergarment, similar to a modern nightgown

circulation—the widespread availability of a magazine, book, or other publication

communally—done together

depression—a period of time with little movement of money and high unemployment

elite—successful and powerful

engraved—carved with fine lines, letters, and designs

epidemic—relating to the widespread outbreak of a disease in a region

governesses—women paid to care for and teach a child or children in a family's home

hygiene—things done to keep yourself and your surroundings clean

idyllic—peaceful and happy

kinship—extreme closeness

morality—beliefs about right and wrong

prescribed—made an official rule

Puritans—members of a Protestant group that disagreed with many teachings of the Church of England and had strict ideas about morality and behavior

segregated—kept apart based on race, gender, ethnicity, or religion

self-reliance—independence

spinsters—older women who have never been married

sterilized—cleaned by destroying germs

suffragette—a woman seeking women's right to vote at a time when women could not

surname—last name; family name

uncannily—in a strange way that's hard to understand

vegan—a person who does not eat any part of an animal or animal-made product, such as milk, eggs, and cheese

vogue—style, fashion, or popularity

Index

abolition, 9–10, 18–19

Alcott, Abigail May, 5

Alcott, Amos Bronson, 4–6, 8, 13, 28–29, 40

antiseptic, 38

Bloomer, Amelia, 34

books, 4–5, 16, 26, 29

Boston, 4, 10

Boston Latin School, 26

cholera, 37–38

Civil War, 10–11, 13, 36

Concord Circle, 8–9

Concord Summer School of Philosophy, 28–29

corset, 32, 34–35

courting, 22

cravat, 31

Declaration of Sentiments, 18–19

Douglass, Frederick, 18

drawers, 31

Emerson, Ralph Waldo, 8–9, 16

Flower Fables, 16

Fruitlands, 40–41

Fuller, Margaret, 9

Gilded Age, 10, 12

Godey's Lady's Book, 21

Good Wives, 12

Hawthorne, Nathaniel, 9

hoop skirt, 32–33

hoops, 24

Hospital Sketches, 10

knickers, 32, 34

Lane, Charles, 40–41

Lister, Joseph, 38

Little Women, 5, 12–13, 15, 16, 29

Lulu, 17

McGuffey Readers, 26

Mott, Lucretia, 18

Nightingale, Florence, 38–39

Pasteur, Louis, 38–39

Pennsylvania, 4

prep school, 27

Puritans, 20

quacks, 38

Seneca Falls, 18

singing school, 23

smallpox, 37

Stanton, Elizabeth Cady, 18–19

Temple School, 29

Thoreau, Henry David, 8–9

Transcendental, 6, 8, 41

tuberculosis, 37

Underground Railroad, 10–11

underwear, 31–32, 34

vegan, 6, 40

Victoria, Queen, 34

weddings, 23

women's rights, 9, 14, 18–19

Check It Out!

This list includes some of Louisa May Alcott's books and their original printing dates.

Eight Cousins (1875)
Good Wives (1869)
Hospital Sketches (1863)
Jo's Boys (1886)
Little Men (1871)
Little Women (1868)
Long Fatal Love Chase, A (1866)
Modern Mephistopheles, A (1877)
Old-Fashioned Girl, An (1870)

Books

Cheever, Susan. 2011. *Louisa May Alcott: A Personal Biography*. Simon & Schuster.

Cheney, Ednah Dow (ed.). 2010. *Louisa May Alcott: Her Life, Letters, and Journals*. Applewood Books.

Krull, Kathleen. 2013. *Louisa May's Battle: How the Civil War Led to* "Little Women." Walker Childrens.

Matteson, John. 2008. *Eden's Outcasts: The Story of Louisa May Alcott and Her Father*. W. W. Norton & Company.

Videos

Armstrong, Gillian. 1994. *Little Women*. Columbia Pictures.

Cukor, George. 1933. *Little Women*. RKO Pictures.

Porter, Nancy. *Louisa May Alcott: The Woman Behind* "Little Women." American Masters, PBS.

Websites

Louisa May Alcott Society. *Louisa May Alcott Society*. http://www.louisamayalcottsociety.org.

Louisa May Alcott's Orchard House. *Louisa May Alcott's Orchard House*. http://www.louisamayalcott.org.

Try It!

Imagine you are a journalist for a newspaper during Louisa May Alcott's lifetime. Choose one of the people mentioned on pages 8–9 to interview for your local paper: Henry David Thoreau, Ralph Waldo Emerson, Margaret Fuller, or Nathaniel Hawthorne.

- Develop 5–10 questions you would like to ask about his or her life, works, and connection to Louisa May Alcott.

- Research your chosen person to develop accurate answers to your interview questions. You may even want to use direct quotations from these important people of the time.

- Design a newspaper layout by hand or on the computer. Create a name for your newspaper. Write your interview and include an eye-catching title.

- You may also want to include other parts of a newspaper along with your interview: smaller feature articles from the time, editorials, advertisements, or a political cartoon.

About the Author

Dona Herweck Rice has written hundreds of books, stories, and essays for kids on all kinds of topics from pirates to heroes to why some people have bad breath! Writing is her passion, but she also loves reading, live theater, dancing any time and anywhere, and singing at the top of her lungs. (Although, she'd be the first to admit that this is not really a pleasure for anyone else). Dona was a teacher and is an acting coach. She lives in Southern California with her husband, two sons, and a cute but very silly little dog.

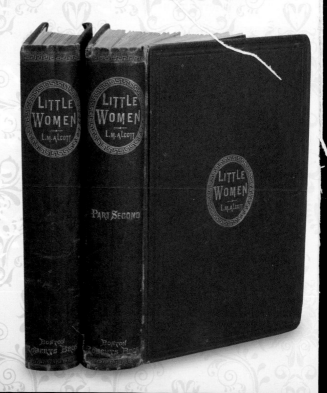